FIVE

Helen Bowell, Prerana Kumar,
Eva Lewis, Laura Potts, Ruth Yates

NEWPOETSLIST

the poetry business

Published 2024 by
New Poets List
The Poetry Business
Campo House,
54 Campo Lane,
Sheffield S1 2EG

Copyright © The Authors 2024
All Rights Reserved

ISBN 978-1-914914-78-2
eBook ISBN 978-1-914914-79-9
Cover design: Jess Rollit
Typeset by Utter
Printed by Biddles Books

Smith|Doorstop Books are a member of Inpress:
www.inpressbooks.co.uk

Distributed by NBN International, 1 Deltic Avenue,
Rooksley, Milton Keynes MK13 8LD

The Poetry Business gratefully acknowledges
the support of Arts Council England.

Contents

HELEN BOWELL

1	Short Biog
1	The World's Smallest Ball of Paint
2	Ketchup
3	Nêspera
5	If You Can Go to Hell for Lust
5	Front Crawl

PRERANA KUMAR

7	Where My Body is Cactus
8	Creation Story
9	I Rewind the Second My Mother's Girlhood Breaks
10	Atonement
12	Legacy Story: Drape
14	Kali Lays Down Her Swords

EVA LEWIS

15	Memories I Ruin / Three Erasure Poems
16	Broken yellow wallpaper / those days
17	A Cave Waters Shadows

LAURA POTTS

19	The Picture in Ireland
20	Sweet Autumn
21	Holly
22	Yesterday's Child
23	But then parts of you
24	Night Song

RUTH YATES

27 School on Saturday
27 Doncaster Pride
29 Mountaintops
29 My Great-great Grandad
30 Otter
31 To Charles Altamont Doyle

33 About the authors
34 Acknowledgments

HELEN BOWELL

Short Biog

Helen is a medium-sized tree with triangle-shaped leaves from Europe. Her work has appeared in Lancashire bobbins, spools and reels; woodlands, downs and heaths; and is forthcoming in gardens in Lapland. She has provided food and habitat for over three hundred insect species and fungi such as fly agaric, woolly milk cap and chanterelle. Her branches have driven out the spirits of the old year, and have symbolised purity, love and fertility, impregnating many cows.

The World's Smallest Ball of Paint
after John Green

I came across the World's Smallest Ball of Paint when driving down the M4 to Bristol on a clear Tuesday morning. The sign for the exit appeared just as I was wondering about my next comfort break, and so I indicated and left the main road. It was exhibited in someone's terraced house, very 50s, patterned wallpaper, Orla Kiely pillowcases and tea cosies. The lady – her name was Joan – put the kettle on and told me about the world's largest ball of paint in America – started off a painted baseball, now the size of a barn – and why are Americans obsessed like that? So she'd decided, with a few friends, to do the opposite – Smallest Ball of Paint, Smallest Ball of Elastic Bands, Smallest Ball of Yarn. The others were in the New Forest and a market town just outside Lincoln, but here we were – did I want milk and sugar – with the World's Smallest Ball of Paint.

That night, in the Premier Inn, I dreamt the day over again, only this time it was the World's Smallest Ball of Pain, and it was being exhibited in my childhood house. I walked with Joan into the living room. Where is it? I said, as she said, They all make that joke, sweetie. It was in the display case facing us, next to photos of the Queen as a young woman and mounted fine china plates. I don't know what to tell you, it was barely there at all.

Ketchup

Dark red school jumper sauce.
Thick, stuck to the bottle's ceiling,
made stickier by force.
Sweet tang on chips, burgers, toast
in Bournemouth breakfast buffets,
parents fighting. Egg fried sandwich and.
Sausage sandwich and.
Butter, pasta and.
In any good spag bol.
Non-Newtonian fluid from
the Cantonese for tomato sauce.

Nêspera

I've never eaten one,
but you're plucking

them from your
parents' garden, telling

me the tart juice
tastes like luck.

In my childhood
bed, I'm reading

about your
favourite fruit,

learning the English
word *loquat*

is a mistake:
a Chinese poet

once took them
for unripe kumquats,

and it stuck.
All my life, I've called

myself nothing, scared
of learning

I'm wrong.
When at last

I take
the fruit

between my
lips, it's not

an apricot,
nor a peach,

but both.
You think I am

a gold-skinned
nêspera –

your word –
which sounds

to my
beginner's ears

like não espere,
like summer's here,

don't wait
any more.

If You Can Go to Hell for Lust

after Hieronymus Bosch

Can I give you this trout for safe-keeping?
Don't look like that, with your hand on my wrist.
I am an owl staring at what I've done.
Will you hide with me in this tight red cone?
Will you carry me on your back when I'm trapped in a clam?
Take me into the trees.
Place a ball in my mouth with your beak.
I am facing the biggest fish of my life.
Put a toad on my chest and touch me.
Put me in a drum and bang me.
Look at that man, skating on ice.
Oh, barman, I'm trying to make this boat go
but I just don't know how.

Front Crawl

after Emily Berry

I go swimming with the barman.
I consider not wearing goggles
so as to appear more sensual and less
like a frog, but I can't take the chlorine.

I have to do lengths. Just a few.
Even if the barman minds,
he'll get used to it.
He assures me he's fine,

but I keep looking back
down the lane to check.
He nearly drowned
when he was fifteen,

the river too fast, the ciders
too quick. His friend dove in,
kick-boxed the current,
and the water let him go.

He says luck didn't come
into it, it wasn't so bad,
he could have swum out of it.
And suddenly I can't see him –

I stop mid-lane,
splash to the side and hoist
my slick self out
to find him laughing. Good joke.

I slide back in and do my very best
breast-stroke, thinking how
the barman couldn't say
what luck was to save his life.

PRERANA KUMAR

Where My Body is Cactus
    For my sister

At least the supple mirage of sisterhood;
a fleshy lap, a string of pulp-flowers in her hair

After that, mehfooz:
her forehead draped by my hand
tracing intricacies of sleep

        But Nani's laceration is her father's milk
        and I am succulent with its curdle

        Did you know Mama's budmouth
        moves in my cheeks, still suckling
        from that darkened breast?

I have become thorned to stomach it,
and still within me the stain is turgid

Let me say one last time
I was harmed

The memory of wetness remains
no matter which body,
no matter how warned

So swollen, I stop bringing her Mama's nightsilk and

        I didn't do it to hurt you jaana,
        I only wanted you unbreakable,
        but when I bend to kiss your hands,
        my tongue is a soaked lash

Creation Story

the land was born from a coconut it fell   cracked and sweetjuice became water   & all that white part
soiled and rooted and flowered and the coconut was from the stomach of the goddess   with her
hair in the swirl of an eeyrie   No they always say the coconut was from not the coconut was from *cut
                                                                                                       out of*
or   a man threw an axe   into the sea and where the axe landed   Kerala rose like a throat
stuffed with fish   No they always say where the axe *landed* not where it *parted her waters*   or
was it a spear from the hand of a greedy king   No it was a warrior sage's rage   No it was the sixth
of the ten avatars and the aim of his birth was to fill five lakes with blood   No   it was a
long line of chieftains who thought they could boil away enough seawater   to lengthen their
                                                                            coastline
and their wives grew bored   waiting for them to come home and began braiding each other's hair
                                              No there were no men

tell it again

                    the rooted Mother tree whispered every day to a Sea she could not touch
         and one day she shed her hair that writhed into snakes and slithered into the ground and wound
             themselves around her roots and carried her into the briny arms of her lover and Yes the Mangroves
                were born from their first touch and soiled and rooted and flowered and Yes the Tree dropped its egg
                   into the Sea in tenderness which fell and cracked one layer and swelled and Yes the water that was let
                        in that first layer became sweetjuice and Yes this is how the land was born from a coconut

Prerana Kumar

I Rewind the Second My Mother's Girlhood Breaks

I am below her when it happens:
she let's go of the banyan's hanging roots,
her body launched into bulbul's arc
on the upswing, so many ixora blooms
clouding through her cheeks

My mouth wants itself a perpetual hole
for laughter to cocoon

>Please, let her rise, let her nest
>into joy

Let her believe her bones remain bird-hollow
in this wind that smells of rosemilk,
let her hear the grinding of cardamom,
a sparrowed lullaby humming the weeds

But here comes the slow fall;
her shoulder in fragments which quill
straight for the thrumming of her chest

I refuse her inheritance,
resent my eagled clavicle, the rasp
in its turn

I want selfishly for grace,
bitter even when she takes care
to play me her cleanest whistling:
how she crawls through her father's carpets,
whispers *udaan* twelve times, rubs

the small of her back into intimate feathers

how she tucks old quills
into the chadar of my forehead,
a fresh hatchling throwing its first chirp
into her filling mouth

She is sorrowed when she brushes my hair,
I tried, but you love me so different
in your dreams

And I am treacherous to forget
what unravels in the afterbreak:
my mama thrown against the sky,
cresting in her stubborn laughter

Keep her there

Atonement

You look for what nana leaves you
as soon as you wake, a heartful
of washed sprouts, softened hibiscus stems,
the rifted shells of snails, a spine
for you to follow to the garden

where you hide behind the moulding ixora, unflowered,
planted the evening he first wept joy as a father,
wanted for your mother a saccharine blooming
that never took

Prerana Kumar

You watch him reach bare-handed,
bend a shaft of kari leaves, then strip it,
one razor leaf at a time
across the long penance of his finger

A bellyful of blood-soaked leaves nestling
in the swaddle of his banyan every morning
since you let slip that there was
a karipatha plant bedded in her garden,
your father a glutton
for fat-crowned curries

a slow rust thread opening
your mother's palm when she crushed
karileaf by the dozen

And you remember how you got here
in a burst:

your mama crying *please,*
please into her hands while from the dingy gut
of the house, her husband swung a smirk
of a knife against a week-old leg
of lamb

then your nana's voice; a whip
through her face

I'm sorry, I can't take you home with me

Legacy Story: Drape

The first time I saw nani drape a saree,
tussar silk shrouding each sorrow
was mama for her brother's wedding,
afterbirth scars silvering the gauze
into thick pleats, a fountain

        of women line their gums with saffron
        before worship, it's modest, nani says

to hide how a body flays
in some kinds of light,
at least they see swaying

        Legend is that dancer Draupadi,
        who might have been peeled by a hundred swords,
        was cocooned instead in yards of velvet,
        woven from a kind god's hands

        until he crumpled into her spinning
        and then began the first unseaming
        of her stitch

Isn't this my first full drape at fifteen,
my papa clapping a table as uncle ramesh said
carve up my wheat body if I look
at him wrong

        Isn't this a man in england asking
        what a pleasing skintone might blush like;
        answer purplestreak, amberspit,
        each mudgirl colour a kind of bruising
        to hide

Prerana Kumar

the darker goats, led to the woods first
by ceremonial scarves, before their bleating
becomes meatwater in the air

When asked if I'm north of the deccan
or south of the plateau, I say four languages
grace my waist-tuck

> Yesterday I soaked through my bandages
> and laughed until all my anklets welted
> in threads

> A daughter escaped the coast a story ago
> in her grandmother's silk

> When she dug out that first bow
> from the base of her neck,
> she found every family woman
> muscled there into knots

Backless every night,
I pleat my grandmother's leftover
body in windows

I tell myself it's for the view
not the fall

Kali Lays Down Her Swords
for fahad and kym
after eugenia leigh

I've been swinging from the high branch for years, so lipped
with violence. What glaciated in me was a prayer bead fractured

mid-prayer. A darkling hymn against my father's hands. Learned love
was another cleaving rim. A promise

of tender made to a body; neem paste soothed onto a scar — then a blade
sunk to the hilt without blinking. That twisted mouth afterward.

And I would've stiffened ice in the winter. Cursed to feel forever my wound
opening against the sharp. Too afraid of love

to move. But you caught my eye across the meadow.
Left me offerings palm-warmed: sparrowbone, seal-tooth, lacewing

scooped by the fist. Stuck your hands straight in there. Unwound
the great hurt of my life into a silken lullaby, hummed back to me

the small coaxing warmth. Everything you burned to keep me
here: tallow candles shored up for the apocalypse, oil fingered from the necks

of heirlooms, cast-iron shavings; rusted precious over the years.
Without asking. Everything you burned

to see me through the long obsidian of my past.
That unrelenting whetstone. I came so bladed

until I didn't. Until you offered up the dappled orchards
of your memory, the cost of heat rising by the week.

Held up a match and said: come,
we built you this fire.

EVA LEWIS

Memories I Ruin / Three Erasure Poems

#1

I was a holiday park in Wales.
My memories forgot to bring teddy bears
and sleep. So my sister won both on arcade
claw machines. Even machines are fixed.
I remember when I took after a day at the beach.
Being fascinated by her naked riots.
And scared because London wasn't answering
her phone. I normally answer the vending machine
and return with change. But lied to memory.
Mixed up in all of I. Swimming alone in the door.
I was cold and raining. I remember free.

#2

I am Autumn with a hostel.
An exhibition of acts
like one big skeleton tattoo.
Broken taught him how to kill
Octopuses. We are crossing busy
dark matter. Want is suddenly terrified
that I'm no. The girl who has beautiful
grabs me softly by the hand.
Her voice makes me go into art.
It is a series of rooms with light
and sound insulations.
One room choreographed our heads.
I felt the floor tightly when she cried.

#3

Last night I could turn into an attack.
I got performance anxiety and couldn't
watch all the people die.

A Harley Davidson motorcycle gets stressed
and likes to ride really fast over the mountains
until the stress fires into orange sunset.

Broken yellow wallpaper / those days

when I would take off / my name lifting
from shoulders before PE
lessons / folding its white collar
in half on the bench / for an hour's rampant blood
temperature / heart rate / elevated without it.

then / its little stitches / almost curling off like damp
wallpaper / handiwork of steri strip / precision in my grand-
mother's needle pointed eyes / i would scuff
it / un sweat stained / numbly dry / pulling over head /
and live with its little / black letters pressing in / to the nape of
my neck / like another thing / I can, now, think of.

A Cave Waters Shadows

i.

Growth too has a curfew. For example a dark
room descending on its stem, spine bending towards rock
-bottom. You do not need to say it more than once for a cave

ii.

to remember. I do not need my mother to repeat
I am a disappointment. I wore a hole
in my shoe. And because nothing truly disappears
I wore the inverse of that hole on my heel for two

iii.

weeks. A blister saturated into a dome. It leaked
when I popped it. Sobbing or drooling. The body after all
is mostly water. The difference between a tsunami and a beach
is the structure

iv.

of earth beneath it. What year 7 lesson isn't Sisyphus
-bound? The mouth spoons each word round as
hunger; a boulder. My mother shoulders her
way up in my thoughts. Again. Ghosts are the same as

v.

the boulder. The absence in a cave is what
echoes. The wind with a snake's tail in it
rattling through this exposed house. Does the sun identify as

vi.

a rock, a planet or somewhere in between light
and ash? I identify as Neptune, all those rings like years

vii.

around my eyes. Ice and rock that could not be contracted
into a planet. I am orbiting the bad

viii.

decisions I made twenty years ago. Insomnia identifies as
purple. The sun a welt raised,

ix.

into a boulder. It is hunger. My mother pushes up
to the precipice of my lungs and dangles

x.

her legs thrashing: a child's swing set. I seesaw on
the verge of tilted earth. I well

xi.

up. My mother shouts down to me, the water. My whole
body rings from her words. A stream circling a dropped penny.

LAURA POTTS

The Picture in Ireland

In the beginning was the bird on the hinge of spring,
and the misting flocks on the knoll's wet chin
fled from the fox with his shot and gun. It was morning.
We sang up the sun with the Sunday hum-and-hymn

of Mam chiming down that patchwork land. Through
the nocturne town and far, past the blackthorn bowed to
prayer and vows that wilted in the air, the city threw
its lights on you. In the darkest heart of Belfast it was 1972.

That dawn of last and longest death, we woke the eyelid
of the day and laid the dark to rest. I remember, kid, the wind
blew like a passing breath and in that way it always did
the forest sang beneath your step. And in the sooner-far ahead,

the meadows fled away from where the dark things slept.
With Dad's flat cap upon your head, coughing through a cigarette
whose end you never met, you ran a mile electric with the planets
in your eyes. You drew the bows of playground boys while I, yes,

the star that fell behind, shook and sweated lemons at the sin
of passing church. You never cared for that. You never tipped
your hat. You laughed and cursed and spat the cleric's
sermons to the last, and that was that. Always just good craic.

But at the blast, beneath the drums of Carthage all the stars
unhinged and fled. And you, kid, who leapt the fire-heart ahead
left only scraps of wind to mark the passage of your death.
For in your last and loudest steps the decades fled beneath your legs,

and past the chapel-arch ahead, a diadem upon your head,
you raised a weeping rag of red. You warned the living of the dead.
And said that prayer you'd never said, but it was lost instead.
And in those gobbet-drops of flesh wept Our Lady overhead.

I waved, and mouthed a broken vowel which you would never see.
And saw you in the longest light, where you will always be.

Sweet Autumn

And years later, you at the bus stop.
Yesterday's leaves in your hair.
The seat where we laughed.
Our words in the air.

Sweetheart. The years threaded up
our names scratched on the glass.
Rain argued away the grass-stained
fingerprints, the love turned over

on clumsy tongues, the moonbows,
the setting suns. My skin soft-tossed
in sheets, hard-kissed. The taste
of your words. The clench of my fist

in the deafening dawn. Oh day,
when the pavement rolled beneath
our feet. Bubblegum from the shop.
My Monet mouth, your Friday chips –

Stop. Darling, how we used to crease
at the waist. Pink and white laughter
poured from our lips. And when I meet
you at the curb of my sleep it is when

we were here, my heart in your hands,
your hands on my dress. They said you
spilt your filth down telephone wires.
Cheap love. Sex. I wouldn't know.

I walked away. Like this. Yes.

Holly

In a suitcase your years at the lit bus stop.
Laughing loud and long, the top
of your lungs a screaming fox,
you had stopped to tell me you were gone.

Yesterday a word dark on your lips. Chips
I remember we split in the rain, a fizzing
last laugh in a childhood lane, smacking
our knees as the trees threw their bats.

Again as the streetlamps hung in their hats
I remembered we dreamed at the back
of a class a lost and dizzy tomorrow.
Remember that? Most of those stars left long ago.

Holly. The river has forgotten your name. No,
your broken light the same to me,

cracked black by the decades we did not see
from your garden gloam. That night as I walked

the last mile home a scrap of your laugh clung
to the wind and your bicycle bell, fifty years long,
thinned to a song I have heard since then, your afterglow
gone. Do you remember the thunder like a great Amen?

I looked on.

Yesterday's Child

The sun slid a knife through the April night
and bled like an egg, like a budburst head.
In the swell of the sweat on the belly of the bed,
broken-throated then and red, you said
the clench of winter let the roses grow instead.

But time has fled with jenny wren and left
the meadow dead. And overhead a mouth of moon
has called a mourning on this room, and soon
an ever-bloom of moss will clot the loss of you.
For the years between us are wide as a child,

and the tears as wet as a wound.

But then parts of you

are dead. I sent the world a postcard from a fusty
window that said
        I am wearing my grief.

Sling clothes into the bin: your socks, your skirts,
the notebook in the pocket of the moth-eaten dress,
        pearls, perfume,

that locket - yes - the one etched with that lover's name
you would never speak, but traced with warmer words
        in the quiet curls

of firelight. Death in his Sunday finery asleep in the hall.
I call. *Mother.* Hear you still singing while washing
        the dishes.

Now. Minds do many things. Canteen food garden gate
passing-bells rings. A wind slips beneath the door and
        I hear you humming,

a voice swollen with the years of rolled-up sleeves
and tired eyes. The cries of a child at its mother's knee.
        See,

I remember Wordsworth, Tennyson, Keats, falling
from your tongue in a hospital bed. *Mother*, I said,
        forty years from

the child in your arms, *there are parts of you dead.*

Laura Potts

Bottle and Bible. Now this is pleasurable. Somewhere
on the other side of the night I am hearing you say
       the fields are alive

when the moon is bowed. Your name is stirring
in the trees and is gone. Just look what you're doing.

Look at me now.

Night Song
    After Anthony Burgess in Manchester

Birds came in on the tail of the day
       to the evening bells of Harpurhey.
Dusk had smudged the land, the lanes
     long as sorrow

               in the graceless rain.

He'll remember the hour –
      the saddening glamour of lamps
in the dark. The way the city lit its quiet lights
     below the stars.

And this is home. Old as coal,
        as cotton. Old as the throat
that a boy broke open there,
           at evensong.

Yes, Manchester.
    The little lights lived on.

He knew the prayers, the silver songs

        that lit the sky by night.

How time would remember this city.
    The thousand lost tomorrows

        and the avenues of light,

and oh
    the human music –

        the everbells, the pipes

that lifted through the smoke
their held, their holy notes.

And those bright gods.
    Over the domes of the dark, he watched
the sparrows charm and sparkle

        into absence, into loss.

RUTH YATES

School on Saturday

She went to school and let herself
into the classroom and started
on the playdough, even though
the colours were rather grey now

and there was nobody around
to notice how she used the cutters
to make all the shapes she wanted.
She already knew how to tie

her shoelaces in a double knot
and stood the stillest in line, only
she didn't realise it wasn't a Saturday
and the classroom was full.

All the windows in the classroom
looked out on to better things.

Doncaster Pride

The security guard sits wearily
on a blue striped deckchair,
here till 10pm, it's alright
but hasn't even started yet.

And a dog barks, a car revs,
people layer rainbow upon
rainbow, in t-shirt flag and badge,
and the woodpigeon still calls

your name, less mournfully now.
It's been a long year and it's only
August. And the woodpigeon
keeps going, never gives up

like one of the five tenets
of Taekwondo. Consider
Courtesy, opening the door
for others, and Integrity,

admitting it was the wrong door
or the wrong others. Perseverance,
the woodpigeon goes on.
Self-Control, not responding

to the provocation of the cat
watching the dog next door,
who is barking until he is sick
and his throat has no bark,

and she sits and watches calmly,
then finally walks away. Indomitable Spirit.

Mountaintops

Oh! When I stepped off the plane
she was an archangel and folded
me in her arms. She stood tall, her hair
all the way down her back, and I remembered

the expression: *non scherzare con le montagne*
and how in Chinese creation myth
mountains used to move around, had wings
until these were cut off by the angry gods.

And she in walking boots and climbing gear
held me and just for that moment
I was in the mountaintops in the snow
and she didn't have to push me to jump

as she had done from the third floor window
when the snow was six feet high
and we all leapt in up to our waists.
And I marvelled, up here in the snow

at the lack of definition: no towns, no cars below,
no eagles today, no vultures tomorrow.

My Great-great Grandad

was a funeral director
with a real horse and carriage.
Apparently, he was a gentle soul.

I can see him trotting along

somewhere in Birmingham,
the Corn Exchange perhaps,
on his day off, taking the horse out
for some not so covert advertising.

I wonder if he kept mints
in the pocket of his waistcoat.
I met him a few years ago
at a museum in York.

My Grandma and Great-Aunt
stopped at one of those life-size figures:
a splendid carriage, black horse,
a man in a suit stood tall,

and my Grandma said:
'He was just like that'.

Otter

They used to swim in Nye Bevan pool,
just before chips. Nicknamed Otter
for their ability to stay at the bottom of the pool
and crawl along it, way before their Taekwondo
years: this was self-control, perseverance,
indomitable spirit. They did want
the attention of the bigger lads, who petted Otter
and held them on their laps, they made a fuss
of Otter and Otter was the youngest,
self-contained. They crawled along

the bottom of the water for several years,
barely resurfacing, until they realised
at some point they needed to act human
and put the ways of the Otter behind them.
They had thought like an Otter, spoken
like an Otter, and perceived things
pretty much as an Otter. They climbed
out of the water, paw after paw,
gave themselves a shake, put a paw
through their whiskers. No one
noticed the change. No one saw Otter.
Only a little girl climbing out of a swimming pool.

To Charles Altamont Doyle
After Joanne Limburg

> *"What can I do?... I would have thought it would be the duty no less than the pleasure of refined Professional Gentlemen to protect men like myself ... and not endorse utterly false conceptions of sanity or Insanity to the detriment of the life and liberty of a harmless gentleman"*
> – Charles Altamont Doyle

Charles, I'm so deeply sorry for what happened to you and I agree
that the Scottish doctors probably misunderstood your humour
and you bewildered them, or perhaps they felt threatened
or genuinely thought it was for the best in all their Victorian

benevolence. But allow me to give you some advice if you want
to get out. Only show them your drawings if they are exact
representations of what they can see as well. Yes, like this crow
sitting on top of the weeping ash. What, they've not seen that either?

So what are they looking at? When a man looks for madness,
he finds it, just like when you seek anything eventually it arrives:
a rainbow or a big storm, a horse rearing up or two ravens flying,
one with a straw in its beak, or mud on your shoes that needs to dry

before you can get it off. Dear Sir, I would love to correspond with you
but I'm two centuries late. Please accept my humble apologies
and this demonstration of respect for your artistry and your sanity,
in no particular order. Yours.

About the authors

HELEN BOWELL is a poet, producer and editor. Her debut pamphlet *The Barman* (Bad Betty Press, 2022) was a Poetry Book Society Choice and tells the story of a relationship with an unnamed barman backwards. A Ledbury Poetry Critic, her poems, reviews and translations have been published in *bath magg, Poetry London, Poetry Wales* and elsewhere. She co-directs Dead [Women] Poets Society, which resurrects women poets through events and online. In 2023/24, Helen ran a project for bi+ poets culminating in *Bi+ Lines*, the first anthology of bi+ poets (*fourteen poems*, 2023). She was The Poetry Society's Education Officer for six years and produced the Poetry Translation Centre's 20th birthday programme of events in 2024.

PRERANA KUMAR (they/them) is an Indian writer based in London. They won the *Rebecca Swift Foundation's Women Poet's Prize* 2022. They were also shortlisted for *The White Review Poet's Prize* 2022. Their work appears in *The Telegraph, Magma, The White Review, The Poetry Review, Prototype,* and *bath magg* among others. Their debut pamphlet, *Ixora* is out with Guillemot Press. They are currently LAHP-funded and reading for a doctorate in Creative Writing at QMUL.

EVA LEWIS is a queer, neurodivergent writer based in Manchester. They are a co-runner of *SINK Magazine* and editor for *Young Identity*, as well as a member of *The Writing Squad* and *Queer Bodies* poetry collective. Their writing has been published by *Broken Sleep Books, A Velvet Giant, Aster Lit, Ice Floe Press* and others.

LAURA POTTS is a writer from West Yorkshire. A recipient of the Foyle Young Poets Award, her work has been published by *Aesthetica, The Moth* and The Poetry Society. Laura became one of the BBC's New Voices in 2017. She was shortlisted for The Manchester Poetry Prize and The Bridport Prize in 2020

RUTH YATES is a poet based in Sheffield. Their poems have been published in anthologies including *Bi+lines: An Anthology of Contemporary Bi+ Poets, Introduction X: The Poetry Business Book of New Poets,* and *Like Flyering for the Revolution: The Verve Anthology of Protest Poems*; and in magazines including *The North, Route 57,* and *Pennine Platform*.

All five members of *Five* are members of The Writing Squad. Please go to https://www.writingsquad.com/ to find out more.

Acknowledgments

HELEN BOWELL
'Nespera' – *Magma*, issue 86, 2023
'If You Can Go to Hell for Lust' – *The Barman* (Bad Betty Press), 2024
'Front Crawl' – *The Barman* (Bad Betty Press), 2024
'Short Biog' has now been published in *The Hongkonger*, an online newspaper, 2024

PRERANA KUMAR
The poem 'Kali Lays Down Her Swords' takes inspiration from Eugenia Leigh's 'I Was Wrong About So Much'. The poems 'Where My Body is Cactus' (first published in *The White Review*), 'I Rewind the Second My Mother's Girlhood Breaks', 'Atonement' and 'Legacy Story: Drape' (first published in *bath magg*) are taken from my pamphlet *Ixora* (Guillemot Press, 2023).

EVA LEWIS
'Cave Water's Shadow' appeared in *aster lit*.

LAURA POTTS
The Fortnightly Review, *Aesthetica*, *The Edward Thomas Fellowship*, *The Moth Magazine*, The Manchester Poetry Prize and *Southword Journal*.

RUTH YATES
'School on Saturday' was highly commended in the Best Single Poem category of the Disabled Poets Prize 2023.
'To Charles Altamont Doyle' is inspired by Joanne Limburg's *Letters to my Weird Sisters: On Autism, Feminism and Motherhood*. The quote by Charles Altamont Doyle is from his diary, dated June 1889, from *The Doyle Diary: The Last Great Conan Doyle Mystery, with a Holmesian Investigation into the Strange and Curious Case of Charles Altamont Doyle* by Michael Baker.

The Poetry Business is grateful to the support and encouragement of Steve Dearden and The Writing Squad in compiling this anthology.